Diet recommendations during acute renal failure (ARF)

Please check these recommendations always with a nutrition consultant, therapist, doctor or dietician. The recipes and the list of ingredients are supporting the conventional medical therapy. The calorie disclosures of fresh ingredients (fruit and vegetables) vary according to quality and time of harvest. The contents were checked by a dietician and a nutrition consultant for the Traditional Chinese Medicine (TCM).

Author:
©2019 Josef Miligui
www.ebns.at

AF285346

Source:
The lists are created from the EBNS database for nutritional counseling. The database is used by dietitians, therapists and doctors for advising the patient / client.

Literature:
The specialist literature and the training documents of the German and Austrian dietary and traditional Chinese medicine serve as a knowledge base. We have used the documents as a basis of knowledge, adapted it to our experience and completed them.
http://di-book.com

Production and publishing:
BoD – Books on Demand, Norderstedt
ISBN: 9783752811339

Diet recommendations for DIETETICS - Protein and electrolyte - kidney - acute renal failure (ARF)

1   Treatment strategy

Protein-standard diet with biologically high-quality protein.
Reduce cooking salt, potassium and phosphorus, if necessary.
Liquid supply as instructed by the doctor.

2   Avoid

Sodium-, potassium- and phosphorus-rich food and drinks.
Biologically low quality protein.

3 Breakfast

4 Snack

5 Lunch

6 Afternoon

7 Dinner

8 Any time

9 Recipes

(rec.) = You can use more.
(little) = You should use less than specified
(omit) = omit.

9.1 Antipasti

Improves blood circulation, anti-inflammatory, relieves pain. Diuretic, promotes digestion, reduces blood pressure, antioxidative, antibacterial, affects anorexia, improves digestion, flatulence, stomach weakness, stimulating.
Cooking time approx. 40 min
1 portion to 740g. / 301kcal. - (carb:0% / prot:0%)
100g.=40,68kcal. / protein 8,24g. fat:16,82g.
µg. - Ph:23,8 Na:3,24 Ka:202,63 Mg:15,42 Ca:21,64 Fe:0,73 Zn:0,24 Col.:0,02 Hsr.:17,4

Quantity of ingredients:
Pepperoni 1 piece / 5g. (yes)
Lemon juice 1 table spoon / 10g. (yes)
Aubergine 1 piece / 300g. (yes)
Tomato 4 pieces / 200g. (yes)
Zucchini 5/8 oz / 200g. (yes)
Lemon peel 1/2 piece / 3g. (yes)
Olive oil 1 table spoon / 15g. (yes)
Basil (fresh) 8 leaves / 5g. (yes)
Salt 1 pinch / 0,5g. (little)
Coriander 1/2 teaspoon / 2g. (yes)

Cooking instructions:
Preheat the oven to 250 degrees Celsius and bake the hot peppers until the bowl becomes dark (about 20 minutes). Cover the hot peppers with a clear film and allow to cool. Peel the skin and cut into strips about 2 cm wide. Cut tomatoes in half and spread with oil in slices of aubergine and bake in the oven at 200 degrees golden brown (about 10 minutes) Fry the zucchini slices in the grill pan (without fat).
Mix everything together, mix the marinade of olive oil, salt and lemon peel and pour over the vegetables, sprinkle with coriander. Leave for 1 hour.

9.2 Apple and celery soup with roasted fennel

Reduces blood pressure, strengthens immune system, strengthens stomach, triggers stagnation, mineral and vitamin rich. Relieves constipation. metabolism-promoting and dehydrating healing effect.
Cooking time approx. 1 hour
Allergens: L
5 portions to 299g. / 191kcal. - (carb:65% / prot:35%)
100g.=63,75kcal. / protein 9,91g. fat:8,32g.
µg. - Ph:12,47 Na:9,59 Ka:40,8 Mg:12,03 Ca:47,53 Fe:0,26 Zn:0,01 Col.:0 Hsr.:6,06

Quantity of ingredients:
Celery root 1 piece / 350g. (yes)
Apple (sour) 1 piece / 175g. (little)
Onion white 1 piece / 100g. (yes)
Rapeseed oil 2 table spoons / 20g. (yes)
Basic recipe for a vegetable soup (nutritious) 2 1/4 cups / 600g. (little)
Fennel 1 piece / 150g. (yes)
Salt 1 pinch / 0,5g. (little)
Pepper (ground) 1 pinch / 0,1g. ()
Soy cream 1/2 cup / 100g. (little)

Cooking instructions:
Peel onion and celery and dice roughly. Peel the apple, quarter, remove the core, cut the apple into cubes.
Heat half of the oil in a large saucepan and fry the onion cubes in a medium heat for 2-3 minutes.
Add pieces of celery and pieces of apple and simmer for 1 minute. Add the vegetable broth according to the basic recipe, boil everything and cook over a low heat for about 45 minutes.
In the meantime, clean the fennel, wash and drain. Finely chop the fennel.
Heat a pan, add remaining oil and roast the fennel cubes in medium heat, stirring constantly, until well browned and tender. Season with salt and pepper and keep warm. Puree the soup ingredients in the broth with a hand blender. Brush apple celery soup through a sieve and pour it back into the pot. Add soy cream and heat everything again for about 1 minute. Season the apple and celery soup with salt and pepper.
Spread in the soup plate and serve garnished with the roasted fennel.

9.3 Apricot and cranberry ice cream

Forces resistance to infections, good to fight oral mucosal inflammation, diarrhea. Has a positive effect on the urinary tract.
Cooking time approx. 5 min
2 portions to 222,5g. / 106kcal. - (carb:91% / prot:9%)
100g.=47,87kcal. / protein 1,9g. fat:0,48g.
µg. - Ph:7,98 Na:0,94 Ka:107,17 Mg:4,69 Ca:8,02 Fe:0,03 Zn:0 Col.:0 Hsr.:8,57

Quantity of ingredients:
Apricots 3/4 lbs / 350g. (little)
Water 1/4 cup / 50g. (yes)
Cranberry 3 table spoons / 45g. (little)

Cooking instructions:
Mix the apricot juice with the cranberry syrup. Fill the juice into little molds, place in the freezer and let it freeze in about 3 hours.

9.4 Asparagus and herb ragout

Diuretic, improves blood circulation, prevents cancer, dissolves stagnation, promotes weight loss. Good to fight immunodeficiency, loss of appetite, flatulence, high blood pressure, depressions, diabetes, diarrhea, stimulates liver function.
Cooking time approx. 30 min
Allergens: GL
4 portions to 465,5g. / 168kcal. - (carb:78% / prot:22%)
100g.=36,14kcal. / protein 7,54g. fat:4,09g.
µg. - Ph:2,55 Na:0,54 Ka:11,94 Mg:2,69 Ca:9,45 Fe:0,06 Zn:0,02 Col.:0 Hsr.:1,09

Quantity of ingredients:
Basic recipe for a vegetable soup (nutritious) 2 cups / 500g. (little)
Lemon peel 1/2 piece / 3g. (yes)
Coriander 1/4 teaspoon / 1g. (yes)
Nutmeg 1 pinch / 0,3g. (yes)
Asparagus (green or white) 1,8 lbs / 800g. (yes)
Parsley 1 Bunch / 125g. (yes)
Crème fraiche cheese 2 table spoons / 30g. (little)
Lemon juice 1 teaspoon / 3g. (yes)
Potato 7/8 lbs / 400g. (little)

Cooking instructions:
Cook potatoes with plenty of salted water about 20 min. until soft.
Heat the vegetable stock with lemon zest, coriander and nutmeg till it
boil. Cook the peeled and sliced asparagus in it.
Drain asparagus in a sieve. Collect the cooking liquid.
In the blender mix 200 g of cooked asparagus (the lower ends), cooking
liquid and parsley to a smooth sauce. Beat the sauce with crème
fraîche until smooth. Add asparagus and heat again and season with
lemon juice, salt and pepper. Serve with the potatoes.

9.5 Asparagus Cream Soup

Diuretic, improves blood circulation, prevents cancer, laxative,
antiparasitic, stimulates liver function, good to fight loss of appetite,
flatulence, rheumatism, heartburn.
Cooking time approx. 45 min
Allergens: ACG
2 portions to 409,5g. / 240kcal. - (carb:21% / prot:79%)
100g.=58,61kcal. / protein 5,2g. fat:19,85g.
µg. - Ph:9,44 Na:1,5 Ka:15,8 Mg:1,6 Ca:6,23 Fe:0,13 Zn:0,08 Col.:9,84 Hsr.:2,42

Quantity of ingredients:
Water 2 cup / 500g. (yes)
Rapeseed oil 3 table spoons / 30g. (yes)
Wheat flour 2 table spoons / 10g. (yes)
Chicken yolk 1 piece / 25g. (yes)
Cow's milk (whole milk 3.5% fat) 1 table spoon / 15g. (little)
Sour cream 15% fat 1 table spoon / 15g. (little)
Pepper (ground) 1 pinch / 0,5g. ()
Nutmeg 1 pinch / 0,5g. (yes)
Lemon juice 1 teaspoon / 2g. (yes)
Parsley 2 table spoons / 20g. (yes)
Salt 1 pinch / 1g. (little)

Cooking instructions:
Wash and peel the asparagus.
Heat water, a little lemon juice and pinch of salt till it boils. Tie the
asparagus spears together.
Add the asparagus peel to the cooking water and bring to the boil.
Add the asparagus and cook on low heat for about 20 minutes.
Then remove the asparagus bunches and pour the broth through a
sieve.
For the roux, heat the oil in a saucepan, add the flour and sauté until it
is colorless, slowly top up with the asparagus sauce and simmer for 10

minutes. Cut the asparagus spears into pieces about 3 cm long and place them to the soup.

Just before serving, bring the soup to the boil again.
Mix the egg yolk with the milk and sour cream.
Remove the pot from the heat and stir in the egg yolk and milk mixture.
Season with pepper and nutmeg, decorate with the chopped parsley and serve immediately.

9.6   Barley mash with berries

Diuretic, forcing spleen, supports urination, laxative, strengthens kidney, promotes digestion, detoxifying, promotes perspiration, reduces blood lipids, stimulates, dissolves stagnation.
Cooking time approx. 2 hours
Allergens: A
5 portions to 318,6g. / 113kcal. - (carb:82% / prot:18%)
100g.=35,34kcal. / protein 4,01g. fat:0,78g.
µg. - Ph:1,47 Na:0,11 Ka:2,69 Mg:0,63 Ca:0,55 Fe:0,02 Zn:0,01 Col.:0 Hsr.:0,48

Quantity of ingredients:
Water 10 cups / 1200g. (yes)
Barley 1 cup / 120g. (yes)
Ginger fresh 2 slices / 2g. (yes)
Cardamom 3 capsules / 1g. (little)
Salt 1 pinch / 1g. (little)
Raspberry 5/8 lbs - 8oz / 250g. (little)
Cocoa 1 pinch / 1g. (little)
Barley malt 1 table spoon / 15g. (yes)
Lemon Balm (fresh) 2-4 leaves / 3g. (yes)

Cooking instructions:
Boil the barley with water, ginger and cardamom pods in a large saucepan. Close pot with a lid and cook over low heat for about 2 hours.

For 2 servings of cooked barley porridge, place about 2 ladles in a bowl. Stir with sunflower seeds, malt, cocoa powder and a pinch of salt. Stir fresh berries into the porridge and serve sprinkled with fresh mint or lemon balm.

Tip: The pre-cooked barley porridge (without fruit) can be stored well in the refrigerator and used for sweet or savory dishes, e.g. with stewed vegetables or fruit seasoned compote.

9.7   Barley mash with plums

Promotes spleen, diuretic, forcing spleen, supports urination, relaxes, reduces internal heat.
Cooking time approx. 25 min
Allergens: AG
5 portions to 289,6g. / 107kcal. - (carb:81% / prot:19%)
100g.=36,88kcal. / protein 3,15g. fat:1,57g.
µg. - Ph:1,2 Na:0,1 Ka:2,2 Mg:0,44 Ca:0,34 Fe:0,01 Zn:0,01 Col.:0,04 Hsr.:0,42

Quantity of ingredients:
Water 10 cups / 1200g. (yes)
Barley 1 cup / 120g. (yes)
Plum 1 cup / 120g. (little)
Butter organic 2 teaspoons / 6g. (yes)
Sugar cane sugar 1/2 teaspoon / 2g. (yes)

Cooking instructions:
Grind coarse the barley and roast it dry. Add hot water, add ginger and cardamom and let it swell to a pulp in low heat. Core the plums and boil for 10 minutes with a little water. At the end, add the stewed plums, a little butter and sweetener.

Variant: If you want to go fast, you can use barley flakes instead of shot.

9.8   Barley mash with steamed pear

Promotes digestion, supports urination, promotes spleen, diuretic, forcing spleen, relaxes, promotes perspiration.
Cooking time approx. 25 min
Allergens: A
5 portions to 305,8g. / 114kcal. - (carb:86% / prot:14%)
100g.=37,21kcal. / protein 3,26g. fat:0,72g.
µg. - Ph:1,16 Na:0,11 Ka:2,09 Mg:0,44 Ca:0,33 Fe:0,01 Zn:0,01 Col.:0 Hsr.:0,42

Quantity of ingredients:
Water 10 cups / 1200g. (yes)
Barley 1 cup / 120g. (yes)
Ginger fresh 2 slices / 2g. (yes)
Cardamom 3 capsules / 1g. (little)
Salt 1 pinch / 1g. (little)
Pear 1 piece / 200g. (little)
Sugar cane sugar 1/2 teaspoon / 5g. (yes)

Cooking instructions:
Grind coarse the barley and roast it dry. Add hot water, add ginger and cardamom and let it swell to a pulp in low heat. Peel and dice the pear and boil for 10 minutes with a little water. At the end, add the stewed pear, a little butter and sweetener.
Variant: If you want to go fast, you can use barley flakes instead of shot.

9.9 Basic recipe for a reissue soup (Congee)

Low fat content, for the drainage of the body overweight and high blood pressure.
Cooking time approx. 2-4 hours
3 portions to 273,33g. / 140kcal. - (carb:90% / prot:10%)
100g.=51,34kcal. / protein 2,96g. fat:0,48g.
µg. - Ph:1,95 Na:0,19 Ka:1,67 Mg:1,14 Ca:0,57 Fe:0,01 Zn:0,02 Col.:0 Hsr.:2,11

Quantity of ingredients:
Rice variety any 1 cup / 120g. (yes)
Water 6 cups / 700g. (yes)

Cooking instructions:
Cook rice and water in a ratio of about 1: 6. The amount of water determines the thickness of the mash (matter of taste).
Put the rice in a saucepan with a heavy lid. It is important to simmer the rice after a short boil on the slightest flame, otherwise it burns.
Boil the rice for 2-4 hours. The longer it cooks, the more it strengthens. If you want to eat the dish for breakfast, you can put the rice on just before bedtime.
To be on the safe side, you should first check the behavior of your pot and cooker under observation for a similar amount of time, so that nothing burns.
Refrigerate for later use.

9.10 Basic recipe for a vegetable soup, nutritious

Reduces blood pressure, strengthens immune system, prevents cancer, forcing spleen, dissolves stagnation, promotes weight loss. Good to fight immunodeficiency, high blood pressure, depressions, diabetes, diarrhea, reduces blood lipids.
Cooking time approx. 2-3 hours
Allergens: L
5 portions to 240,6g. / 48kcal. - (carb:0% / prot:0%)
100g.=19,87kcal. / protein 1,56g. fat:1,31g.
µg. - Ph:4,86 Na:3,67 Ka:25,68 Mg:1,8 Ca:6,32 Fe:0,1 Zn:0,05 Col.:0 Hsr.:2,78

Quantity of ingredients:
Olive oil 1 table spoon / 4g. (yes)
Onion white 1 piece / 60g. (yes)
Carrot 3 pieces / 200g. (yes)
Parsnip 3/8 lbs - 6oz / 150g. (yes)
Celery root 1 cup / 100g. (yes)
Ginger fresh 1/2 teaspoon / 2g. (yes)
Lemon 1/2 piece / 25g. (yes)
Juniper berry 6 pieces / 6g. (yes)
Thyme dried 1 pinch / 1g. (yes)
Lovage 1 table spoon / 3g. (yes)
Bay leaf 2 leaves / 1g. (yes)
Salt 1 pinch / 1g. (little)
Water 3 cups / 650g. (yes)

Cooking instructions:
Cut the vegetables into cubes.
Heat oil in hot pot, fry shortly onions and vegetables.
Add cold water, then add ginger, bay leaf and lemon juice.
Season with juniper, thyme and lovage. Cover for 2 - 3 hours on a low heat and simmer.
The used vegetables should be thrown away.
The basic recipe serves as a soup base and to refine vegetables, legumes or cereals.
If you want to eat vegetable soup immediately, add the desired vegetables half an hour before.
Refrigerate for later use.

9.11 Black root with yogurt

Stimulates kidney, bladder and forces the cleaning of the body. In the physiological sense, they generally stimulate the glands in the organism. Good to fight acute or chronic constipation of the intestine. Rich in Vitamins and trace elements.
Cooking time approx. 20 min
Allergens: AG
2 portions to 303g. / 266kcal. - (carb:77% / prot:23%)
100g.=87,95kcal. / protein 7,92g. fat:2,06g.
µg. - Ph:45,47 Na:46,64 Ka:135,46 Mg:13,05 Ca:29,93 Fe:1,29 Zn:0,23 Col.:0,33
Hsr.:28,98

Quantity of ingredients:
Salsify 1 lbs / 400g. (yes)
Yogurt (natural, 1.5% fat) 4 table spoons / 80g. (yes)
Salt 1 pinch / 1g. (little)
Multi-grain bread (gray bread) 6 slices / 120g. (yes)
Herbs various 1 handful / 5g. (yes)

Cooking instructions:
Peel the salsify and simmer in salted water until tender. Pour away the water, cool the salsify and cut it to size. Cover with yoghurt and sprinkle with fresh herbs. Serve with the bread.
You can also use the salsify from the conserve.

9.12 Blueberry puree

Bilberry is laxative. Clove dissolves stagnation. Cinnamon powder heats stomach and spleen, improves blood circulation.
Cooking time approx. 10 min
1 portion to 271g. / 10kcal. - (carb:78% / prot:22%)
100g.=3,69kcal. / protein 0,2g. fat:0,32g.
µg. - Ph:0,98 Na:1 Ka:5,56 Mg:1,09 Ca:6 Fe:0,06 Zn:0,1 Col.:0 Hsr.:1,48

Quantity of ingredients:
Blueberry 1/2 oz / 20g. (little)
Cinnamon ground 1 pinch / 0,1g. (little)
Clove 1 piece / 1g. (yes)
Water 1 cup / 250g. (yes)

Cooking instructions:
Boil blueberries with cinnamon and clove in water for 10 minutes. Remove the cinnamon and clove. Puree. Sweet as desired.

9.13 Broccoli cream soup

Strengthen your immune system, build and maintain healthy bones, teeth, hair and nails. Reduces blood pressure, strengthens immune system, prevents cancer, reduces radiation damage.
Cooking time approx. 30 min
Allergens: LO
6 portions to 251,17g. / 98kcal. - (carb:79% / prot:21%)
100g.=39,02kcal. / protein 4,17g. fat:1,91g.
µg. - Ph:1,14 Na:0,45 Ka:4,37 Mg:1,39 Ca:5,42 Fe:0,03 Zn:0,01 Col.:0 Hsr.:0,45

Quantity of ingredients:
Olive oil 2 table spoons / 7g. (yes)
Broccoli 1,1 lbs / 500g. (little)
Carrot 2 pieces / 150g. (yes)
Potato 2 pieces / 120g. (little)
Onion white 1 piece / 50g. (yes)
Water 1 cup / 50g. (yes)
Basic recipe for a vegetable soup (nutritious) 2 cup / 500g. (little)
White wine 1/2 cup / 125g. (little)
Sage 1 teaspoon / 2g. (yes)
Rosemary 1 teaspoon / 2g. (yes)
Pepper (ground) 1 pinch / 0,5g. ()
Salt 1 pinch / 1g. (little)

Cooking instructions:
Add the olive oil to the pan, add the washed and cut broccoli, diced carrots and potatoes, sauté for a short time, add the chopped onion, fill with water, enough water to cover the vegetables at least 3 finger breadths. Add bouillon, salt, add a little bit of white wine, add the seasoned sage and rosemary.
Heat till it boils and then simmer on a small fire for about 25 minutes. Season with pepper, if necessary season with sea salt. Purée the soup.

9.14 Celery and potato cream soup

Reduces blood pressure, strengthens immune system, promotes weight loss. Good to fight immunodeficiency, loss of appetite, flatulence, depressions, diabetes, diarrhea, improves digestion.
Cooking time approx. 45 min
Allergens: GL
4 portions to 241,5g. / 113kcal. - (carb:83% / prot:17%)
100g.=46,69kcal. / protein 2,15g. fat:5,52g.
µg. - Ph:5,96 Na:3,46 Ka:23,98 Mg:22,27 Ca:83,51 Fe:0,18 Zn:0,01 Col.:0 Hsr.:1,49

Quantity of ingredients:
Olive oil 1 table spoon / 10g. (yes)
Onion white 1/2 piece / 25g. (yes)
Basic recipe for a vegetable soup (nutritious) 3 cups / 700g. (little)
Nutmeg 1 pinch / 0,5g. (yes)
Ground 1 pinch / 0,5g. (yes)
Lemon peel 1/4 piece / 1g. (yes)
Crème fraiche cheese 2 table spoons / 20g. (little)
Salt 1 pinch / 1g. (little)
Parsley 1 table spoon / 8g. (yes)

Cooking instructions:
Heat the olive oil in a saucepan lightly. Fry the onions very gently in a mild heat. Pour with vegetable stock according to the basic recipe. Cover and cook for 15 minutes.
Add curd-cut potato, celery, nutmeg, cumin and lemon zest. Spice with salt and cook for 12 minutes. Potatoes and celery should be soft. Remove the lemon peel.
Puree the soup with crème fraiche using a blender. Season the soup with salt.
Arrange the soup in portions with the chopped parsley.

9.15 Chicory salad with tangerine

Dissolves mucus, is rich in A-B-C Vitamins, promotes digestion, forcing spleen, promotes weight loss. Good to fight loss
of appetite, flatulence, immunodeficiency.
Cooking time approx. 10 min
Allergens: AGNO
3 portions to 285g. / 257kcal. - (carb:75% / prot:25%)
100g.=90,06kcal. / protein 5,49g. fat:7,73g.
µg. - Ph:8,6 Na:15,26 Ka:56,29 Mg:4 Ca:9,42 Fe:0,13 Zn:0,04 Col.:0,01 Hsr.:7,09

Quantity of ingredients:
Tangerine 4 pieces / 300g. (little)
Chicory 2-3 pieces / 300g. (yes)
Sesame oil 2 table spoons / 18g. (little)
Pepper (ground) 1 pinch / 0,5g. ()
Salt 1 pinch / 1g. (little)
Vinegar Aceto Balsamico 2 teaspoons / 6g. (yes)
Lemon 1/2 piece / 25g. (yes)
Orange 1/2 piece / 70g. (yes)
Peppers powder 1 pinch / 1g. (little)
Orange jam 1 teaspoon / 4g. (little)
Cream, sweet 30% 1 table spoon / 10g. (little)
White bread (wheat bread) 6 slices / 120g. (yes)

Cooking instructions:
Peel tangerines and cut into bite-sized pieces; Cut chicory roughly and mix well.
Dressing: sesame oil, pepper, salt, raspberry vinegar or balsamic vinegar, a little lemon or orange juice, rose paprika, orange marmalade or, alternatively, another jam, stir well. Give a little sweet cream over the salad and let it pass briefly.

9.16 Compote from apples

Apple (sweet) stops diarrhea, promotes digestion, appetizing, harmonizes the stomach. Warms stomach and spleen, improves blood circulation.
Cooking time approx. 10 min
2 portions to 220,5g. / 67kcal. - (carb:96% / prot:4%)
100g.=30,39kcal. / protein 0,24g. fat:0,45g.
µg. - Ph:1,41 Na:0,51 Ka:18,22 Mg:0,9 Ca:2,16 Fe:0,07 Zn:0,02 Col.:0 Hsr.:1,87

Quantity of ingredients:
Apple (sweet) 1 piece / 220g. (little)
Water 1 1/2 cups / 220g. (yes)
Cinnamon ground 1 pinch / 1g. (little)

Cooking instructions:
Cook the apples (organic) with the skin and seeds. Sprinkle with cinnamon.

9.17 Compote from rhubarb

Antipyretic, analgesic, detoxifying, bactericide.
Cooking time approx. 15 min
1 portion to 230g. / 48kcal. - (carb:92% / prot:8%)
100g.=20,87kcal. / protein 0,64g. fat:0,1g.
µg. - Ph:11,22 Na:1,7 Ka:119,43 Mg:6,43 Ca:25,43 Fe:0,28 Zn:0,15 Col.:0 Hsr.:2,61

Quantity of ingredients:
Rhubarb 1/4 lbs - 4oz / 100g. (little)
Water 1 cup / 120g. (yes)
Honey 1 table spoon / 10g. (yes)

Cooking instructions:
Wash rhubarb and cut small. Boil in the water. Allow to cool a little and add the honey.

9.18 Compote of pears

Pear benefits digestion, supports urination. Cocoa forces liver, strengthens the muscles, strengthens the defense. Good to fight fungi infections.
Cooking time approx. 10 min
4 portions to 270,75g. / 122kcal. - (carb:93% / prot:7%)
100g.=45,24kcal. / protein 1,27g. fat:0,86g.
µg. - Ph:0,76 Na:0,11 Ka:6,01 Mg:0,38 Ca:0,62 Fe:0,01 Zn:0,01 Col.:0 Hsr.:0,69

Quantity of ingredients:
Water 1 cup / 280g. (yes)
Pear 4 pieces / 800g. (little)
Anise (Common Fennel) 1/2 teaspoon / 1g. (yes)
Vanilla pod 1 pinch / 1g. (yes)
Chili (pod or ground) very little / 0,2g. (yes)
Cocoa 1 pinch / 1g. (little)

Cooking instructions:
Boil pears (organic - with peel), aniseed, vanilla, chili soft. Sprinkle with cocoa.

9.19 Corn coffee with cardamom

Diuretic, forcing spleen, supports urination, relaxes, reduces fat.
Cooking time approx. 5 min
1 portion to 136g. / 3kcal. - (carb:99% / prot:1%)
100g.=2,21kcal. / protein 0,11g. fat:0,08g.
µg. - Ph:1,29 Na:1,02 Ka:7,9 Mg:2,49 Ca:5,37 Fe:0,08 Zn:0,09 Col.:0 Hsr.:0

Quantity of ingredients:
Cereal coffee 1 table spoon / 15g. (yes)
Cardamom 2 cores / 1g. (little)
Water 1 cup / 120g. (yes)

Cooking instructions:
Boil water, coffee, sugar and cardamom. Let it set for one min before drinking.

9.20 Cranberry juice

Antibacterial, good to fight loss of appetite, arteriosclerosis, bladder infections, diarrhea, colds. Antipyretic, against free radicals, gout, diuretic, stomach ulcers, oral mucosa inflammation, rheumatism.
Cooking time approx. 5 min
1 portion to 160g. / 43kcal. - (carb:98% / prot:2%)
100g.=26,88kcal. / protein 0,14g. fat:0,02g.
µg. - Ph:2,06 Na:1,53 Ka:11,69 Mg:1,16 Ca:4,22 Fe:0,09 Zn:0,09 Col.:0 Hsr.:3,12

Quantity of ingredients:
Cranberries 2 table spoons / 25g. (little)
Water 1 cup / 125g. (yes)
Honey 1 table spoon / 10g. (yes)

Cooking instructions:
Mix the cranberries with a little water with the blender to a pulp. Add the remaining water and sweeten with the honey.

9.21 Cucumber salad

Diuretic, detoxifying, suppresses conversion of sugar into fat, lowers cholesterol, prevents cancer. Cucumber cools and moistens. Dill works against flatulence, anticonvulsant in gastrointestinal discomfort.
Cooking time approx. 5 min
Allergens: O
2 portions to 206g. / 27kcal. - (carb:68% / prot:32%)
100g.=13,11kcal. / protein 1,61g. fat:0,4g.
µg. - Ph:5,92 Na:2,32 Ka:35,15 Mg:2,16 Ca:4,03 Fe:0,12 Zn:0,05 Col.:0 Hsr.:1,94

Quantity of ingredients:
Cucumber 1 piece / 400g. (yes)
Salt 1 pinch / 1g. (little)
Dill 1 pinch / 1g. (yes)
Vinegar (Apple vinegar) 1 table spoon / 10g. (yes)

Cooking instructions:
Cut the cucumber (do not peel the BIO) thinly and season.

9.22 Cucumber soup

Diuretic, detoxifying, suppresses conversion of sugar into fat, lowers cholesterol, prevents cancer, promotes digestion, diaphoretic, dries out, good to fight yeast infections.
Cooking time approx. 20 min
Allergens: M
4 portions to 235,25g. / 96kcal. - (carb:22% / prot:78%)
100g.=40,6kcal. / protein 0,91g. fat:9,03g.
µg. - Ph:2,67 Na:1,28 Ka:15,6 Mg:1,17 Ca:2,57 Fe:0,06 Zn:0,01 Col.:0 Hsr.:0,85

Quantity of ingredients:
Olive oil 2 table spoons / 35g. (yes)
Cucumber 2 pieces / 400g. (yes)
Water 2 cup / 500g. (yes)
Sage 3 leaves / 3g. (yes)
Mustard 1/2 teaspoon / 0,5g. (little)
Coriander 1 pinch / 1g. (yes)
Cardamom 1 pinch / 1g. (little)
Salt 1 pinch / 1g. (little)

Cooking instructions:
Heat oil and roast short the small cucumbers. Add Mustard seeds, coriander, cardamom and salt. Add water. Simmer for 10-15 min. Puree and decorate with fresh chopped sage.

9.23 Delicately spiced zucchini with tomatoes

Diuretic, promotes digestion, helps to digest fat, reduces blood pressure, dissolves stagnation, antioxidative, supports urination, diuretic, warming the body from the inside, expands blood vessels.
Cooking time approx. 10 min
4 portions to 396,5g. / 203kcal. - (carb:72% / prot:28%)
100g.=51,2kcal. / protein 5,38g. fat:6,62g.
µg. - Ph:10,4 Na:0,79 Ka:35,33 Mg:6,3 Ca:5,58 Fe:0,26 Zn:0,02 Col.:0 Hsr.:5,53

Quantity of ingredients:
Olive oil 1 table spoon / 20g. (yes)
Onion white 2 pieces / 120g. (yes)
Zucchini 4 pieces / 800g. (yes)
Oregano dried 1 pinch / 1g. (yes)
Basil (fresh) 6-8 leaves / 3g. (yes)
Salt 1 pinch / 1g. (little)
Tomato 2 pieces / 120g. (yes)
Rice (whole grain) 1 cup / 120g. (yes)
Water 6 cups / 400g. (yes)
Salt 1 pinch / 1g. (little)

Cooking instructions:
In a hot pan, fry olive oil, finely chopped onions and finely chopped zucchini until half cooked. Add plenty of dried oregano. Salt and chop the tomatoes for a few minutes until the zucchini are tender but crisp. Add fresh basil as desired.
Variation: Put some sheep's cheese over the tomatoes and finish cooking with the lid closed.
Place the rice in salted water, heat till it boils and let it simmer over low heat for about 15 minutes.

9.24 Frozen pineapple juice

Pineapple reduce inflammation, supports urination, cleans the skin.
Cooking time approx. 1 1/2 hours
1 portion to 50g. / 29kcal. - (carb:95% / prot:5%)
100g.=58kcal. / protein 0,25g. fat:0,1g.
µg. - Ph:9 Na:2 Ka:173 Mg:17 Ca:16 Fe:0,4 Zn:0,3 Col.:0 Hsr.:7

Quantity of ingredients:
Pineapple 1/8 lbs - 2oz / 50g. (little)

Cooking instructions:
Juice pineapple yourself or freeze the organic pineapple juice in small portions and if necessary suck.

9.25 Fruit juice

Stops diarrhea, promotes digestion, appetizing, harmonizes the stomach, relieves pain, detoxifying, reduces blood pressure, strengthens immune system, prevents cancer, reduces radiation damage.
Cooking time approx. 10 min
2 portions to 305g. / 176kcal. - (carb:93% / prot:7%)
100g.=57,54kcal. / protein 1,89g. fat:0,9g.
µg. - Ph:4,99 Na:2,24 Ka:37,45 Mg:2,36 Ca:6,04 Fe:0,21 Zn:0,05 Col.:0 Hsr.:4,3

Quantity of ingredients:
Orange 2 pieces / 150g. (yes)
Apple (sweet) 4 pieces / 300g. (little)
Carrot 2 pieces / 150g. (yes)
Honey 1 table spoon / 10g. (yes)

Cooking instructions:
Peel oranges and carrots. Cut all ingredients into cubes so that they fit into the juicer and juice. Sweet with honey.

9.26 Grapefruit juice

Promotes digestion, lowers blood glucose, dries out, provides Vitamin C
Cooking time approx. 5 min
1 portion to 250g. / 107kcal. - (carb:0% / prot:0%)
100g.=42,8kcal. / protein 1,5g. fat:0,5g.
µg. - Ph:17 Na:2 Ka:180 Mg:10 Ca:18 Fe:0,3 Zn:0,2 Col.:0 Hsr.:15

Quantity of ingredients:
Grapefruit (Pomelo) 1 cup / 250g. (yes)

Cooking instructions:
Juice fresh grapefruit or use organic juice.

9.27 Grated apple

Eat 3 times a day - Apple (sour) scraped and brown is stuffing. Relieves diarrhea.
Cooking time approx. 10 min
1 portion to 200g. / 120kcal. - (carb:94% / prot:6%)
100g.=60kcal. / protein 0,6g. fat:0,8g.
µg. - Ph:11 Na:3 Ka:144 Mg:6 Ca:7 Fe:0,5 Zn:0,1 Col.:0 Hsr.:15

Quantity of ingredients:
Apple (sour) 1 piece / 200g. (little)

Cooking instructions:
Peel apple and grate as fine as possible. Leave for at least 5 minutes until it turns brown.

9.28 Melanzani with olive oil and turmeric

Improves blood circulation, reduces inflammation, relieves pain, promotes digestion, helps to digest fat, supports urination, reduces blood pressure.
Cooking time approx. 30 min
Allergens: A
2 portions to 321,5g. / 432kcal. - (carb:47% / prot:53%)
100g.=134,37kcal. / protein 6,13g. fat:30,66g.
µg. - Ph:6,14 Na:10,38 Ka:42,8 Mg:2,74 Ca:3,55 Fe:0,09 Zn:0,05 Col.:0,02 Hsr.:4,84

Quantity of ingredients:
Aubergine 2 pieces / 300g. (yes)
Olive oil 4 table spoons / 60g. (yes)
Tomato 4 pieces / 200g. (yes)
Turmeric (yellow root) 1/2 teaspoon / 1g. (little)
Ground 1 pinch / 1g. (yes)
Salt 1 pinch / 1g. (little)
White bread (wheat bread) 4 slices / 80g. (yes)

Cooking instructions:
Cut the Melanzani into slices and spread them with the tomatoes on a baking tray. Sprinkle with olive oil and then with turmeric, caraway and salt. Bake them in the tube 20 min.
Serve with the white bread.

9.29 Oatmeal soup with spring onion and carrots

Reduces blood pressure, strengthens immune system, prevents cancer, reduces radiation damage, stimulates digestion, reduces pain, stimulates appetite, dissolves stagnation.
Cooking time approx. 30 min
Allergens: AG
3 portions to 266,33g. / 135kcal. - (carb:65% / prot:35%)
100g.=50,56kcal. / protein 3,87g. fat:5,59g.
µg. - Ph:3,67 Na:1,03 Ka:7,89 Mg:1,41 Ca:2,55 Fe:0,1 Zn:0,05 Col.:0,5 Hsr.:1,63

Quantity of ingredients:
Oat 6 table spoons / 48g. (yes)
Carrot 2 pieces / 200g. (yes)
Butter organic 1 table spoon / 15g. (yes)
Nutmeg 1 pinch / 1g. (yes)
Lovage 1 stem / 15g. (yes)
Onion (spring onion) 2 pieces / 40g. (yes)
Water 2 cup / 480g. (yes)

Cooking instructions:
Roast the oats in butter, add salt and spices, pour in water and heat till it boils. After 10 min. add the grated carrots
and lovage, cook for 10 minutes. Finely add chopped onion.

9.30 Pear juice

Promotes digestion, supports urination.
Cooking time approx. 5 min
2 portions to 300g. / 180kcal. - (carb:93% / prot:7%)
100g.=60kcal. / protein 1,8g. fat:1,2g.
µg. - Ph:7,5 Na:1 Ka:62,5 Mg:3,5 Ca:4,5 Fe:0,15 Zn:0,05 Col.:0 Hsr.:7,5

Quantity of ingredients:
Pear 3 pieces / 600g. (little)

Cooking instructions:
Peel pears thinly (vitamins under the skin) and core. Juice in the juicer.

9.31 Polenta with peach

Relieves fatigue, forcing spleen, diuretic, strengthens the defense, good to fight fungi infections, lets urine and bile juice flow, prevents the aging process, strengthens brain cells.
Cooking time approx. 20 min
3 portions to 254g. / 197kcal. - (carb:89% / prot:11%)
100g.=77,56kcal. / protein 4,48g. fat:0,6g.
µg. - Ph:2,76 Na:0,12 Ka:11,83 Mg:0,93 Ca:1,02 Fe:0,05 Zn:0,02 Col.:0 Hsr.:1,56

Quantity of ingredients:
Water 1 1/2 cups / 240g. (yes)
Corn Grease (Polenta) 1 cup / 120g. (yes)
Peaches 2-3 pieces / 400g. (little)
Vanilla pod 1 pinch / 1g. (yes)
Chili (pod or ground) 1 pinch / 0,1g. (yes)
Cinnamon ground 1 pinch / 1g. (little)

Cooking instructions:
Pour the polenta into a pan of hot water with constant stirring until the polenta has the desired consistency. Pull the
polenta from the fire and let it soak for 10 minutes.
Wash fresh peaches and cut into quarters. Pour into the finished polenta the peaches, add the vanilla and add Chili
to taste, stir and let it go for 3 minutes.
Winter varieties: Pickled fruit, pear, apples.

9.32 Potato with dandelion salad

Promotes spleen, reduces inflammation, improves digestion, regenerates skin, supports urinating, lowers cholesterol, detoxifying, reduces inflammation, forcing spleen and digestive system, detoxifying, dissolves stagnation.
Cooking time approx. 25 min
2 portions to 203g. / 162kcal. - (carb:70% / prot:30%)
100g.=79,8kcal. / protein 4,28g. fat:5,59g.
µg. - Ph:26,58 Na:13,03 Ka:176,11 Mg:11,88 Ca:27,41 Fe:0,61 Zn:0,28 Col.:0,01 Hsr.:14,22

Quantity of ingredients:
Potato 5/8 lbs - 8oz / 250g. (little)
Onion white 1/2 piece / 20g. (yes)
Sunflower oil 1 table spoon / 10g. (little)
Dandelion (young plants) 1/4 lbs - 4oz / 125g. (yes)
Salt 1 pinch / 1g. (little)
Pepper white (ground) 1 pinch / 0,5g. (yes)

Cooking instructions:
Cook the potatoes in salted water and cut into thin slices. Finely chop
the onion. Now season the potatoes with oil, salt and pepper and add
the dandelion and mix.

9.33 Pumpkin slices with spicy rice

Strengthens lungs and spleen, diuretic, reduces blood glucose, protects
liver, for the drainage of the body overweight and high blood pressure,
harmonizes liver.
Cooking time approx. 45 min
Allergens: AG
4 portions to 260,5g. / 438kcal. - (carb:59% / prot:41%)
100g.=168,04kcal. / protein 4,2g. fat:27,77g.
µg. - Ph:4,8 Na:1,27 Ka:11,64 Mg:2,02 Ca:3,02 Fe:0,04 Zn:0,02 Col.:0,25 Hsr.:1,33

Quantity of ingredients:
Clarified butter 1/2 teaspoon / 5g. (yes)
Saffron 1 Sachet / 0,1g. (little)
Turmeric (yellow root) 1 teaspoon / 2g. (little)
Rice Basmati 1 cup / 120g. (yes)
Water 1 cup / 120g. (yes)
Salt 1/2 teaspoon / 2g. (little)
Pumpkin 6-8 slices / 400g. (yes)
Barley flour 1 cup / 10g. (yes)
Breadcrumbs (wheat bread, bread roll) 1 cup / 10g. (yes)
Salt 1/2 teaspoon / 2g. (little)
Pepper (ground) 1 pinch / 1g. ()
Butter organic 1 table spoon / 10g. (yes)
Cream, sweet 30% 1 1/2 cup / 300g. (little)
Barley flour 2 table spoons / 20g. (yes)
Chives 3 table spoons / 20g. (yes)
Dill 3 table spoons / 20g. (yes)

Cooking instructions:
Melt the fat in a small saucepan, add saffron and turmeric, lightly roast over medium heat for about 1-2 minutes to allow the aromas to develop (note: the spices should never be burnt). Add the rice for about 2 minutes stir fry, add the salt, stir briefly and add the water, stir and close the pot with a lid. Cook at low to medium heat until the water is almost completely absorbed, then remove from the heat and set aside with the lid still closed and let it swell. Do not stir! When the water is completely absorbed, the rice is ready!

Mix flour, bread crumbs, salt and pepper. Moisten the pumpkin slices with water or mashed egg, turn the slices in the flour mixture and fry gently in butter until golden brown and the pumpkin is soft. Melt the butter in a small saucepan, brown the barley flour in it and remove from heat, add the sour cream, season with salt, pepper, add the chopped herbs and pour the sauce over the fried pumpkin slices. Serve with the rice.

9.34 Pumpkin soup

Promotes digestion, forcing spleen and stomach, reduces blood pressure, strengthens immune system, prevents cancer, reduces radiation damage, improves digestion, regenerates skin, lowers cholesterol, reduces blood glucose, protects liver.
Cooking time approx. 1 hour
3 portions to 236,33g. / 105kcal. - (carb:71% / prot:29%)
100g.=44,29kcal. / protein 2,54g. fat:3,64g.
µg. - Ph:4,02 Na:0,96 Ka:24,72 Mg:1,82 Ca:2,89 Fe:0,08 Zn:0,02 Col.:0 Hsr.:1,08

Quantity of ingredients:
Pumpkin 3/4 lbs / 300g. (yes)
Carrot 2 pieces / 100g. (yes)
Potato 2 pieces / 120g. (little)
Olive oil 1 table spoon / 10g. (yes)
Onion white 1 piece / 50g. (yes)
Water 1 cup / 120g. (yes)
Parsley 1 table spoon / 7g. (yes)
Anise (Common Fennel) 1 pinch / 1g. (yes)
Salt 1 pinch / 1g. (little)

Cooking instructions:
Add the olive oil to the pan, add the diced pumpkin, diced carrots and potatoes. Roast them shortly, add the finely chopped onion, fill with water, add enough water to cover the vegetables at least 3 finger-

widths. Boil at low heat.
Season with sea salt, add small cutted parsley, a pinch of anise (little).
Allow to simmer for about 35 minutes. Then purée the soup and add
some water, depending on the consistency of
the soup.

9.35 Pumpkin-yoghurt soup

Relaxes, reduces blood pressure, strengthens immune system,
promotes weight loss. Good to fight immunodeficiency, loss of appetite,
flatulence, depressions, diabetes, diarrhea.
Cooking time approx. 15 min
Allergens: GL
4 portions to 239g. / 68kcal. - (carb:83% / prot:17%)
100g.=28,45kcal. / protein 2,37g. fat:1,31g.
µg. - Ph:1,79 Na:0,9 Ka:6,6 Mg:2,8 Ca:10,96 Fe:0,02 Zn:0,01 Col.:0,05 Hsr.:0,35

Quantity of ingredients:
Basic recipe for a vegetable soup (nutritious) 1 cup / 300g. (little)
Hokkaido pumpkin 1,1 lbs / 500g. (yes)
Ginger fresh 1/2 teaspoon / 2g. (yes)
Fennel seeds ground 1/2 teaspoon / 1g. (yes)
Anise (Common Fennel) 1/4 teaspoon / 1g. (yes)
Yogurt (natural, 1.5% fat) 3/8 lbs - 6oz / 150g. (yes)
Peppermint 2 leaves / 1g. (yes)
Salt 1 pinch / 1g. (little)

Cooking instructions:
Heat the vegetable broth (after the basic recipe) till it boils. Add diced
pumpkin, chopped ginger, crushed fennel seeds and anise. Bring the
soup to the boil and simmer for about 12 minutes until the pumpkin is
soft.
Remove soup from the heat. Puree the soup with the yoghurt with the
blender. Serve soup with finely chopped mint sprinkled.

9.36 Quick zucchini soup

Diuretic, supports urination. Strengthens gastrointestinal function,
expands blood vessels, prevents cancer, prevents diseases (in the
elderly). Stimulates liver function, detoxifying.
Cooking time approx. 10 min
4 portions to 241,5g. / 42kcal. - (carb:46% / prot:54%)
100g.=17,29kcal. / protein 1,76g. fat:2,04g.
µg. - Ph:3,81 Na:0,41 Ka:29,78 Mg:3,2 Ca:5,37 Fe:0,21 Zn:0,01 Col.:0 Hsr.:2,85

Quantity of ingredients:
Zucchini 2-3 pieces / 500g. (yes)
Onion white 1 piece / 50g. (yes)
Corn germ oil 2 table spoons / 6g. (yes)
Parsley 1 table spoon / 7g. (yes)
Chives 1 teaspoon / 3g. (yes)
Water 2 cup / 400g. (yes)

Cooking instructions:
Fry chopped onion in oil. Add sliced zucchini and sauté well. Pour with water. Chop parsley and chives, add and puree everything.

9.37 Refreshing cucumber soup with potatoes

Diuretic, detoxifying, suppresses conversion of sugar into fat, lowers cholesterol, prevents cancer, reduces inflammation, improves digestion, lowers cholesterol, dissolves stagnation, improves blood circulation, stimulates appetite.
Cooking time approx. 15 min
Allergens: GN
3 portions to 307,33g. / 148kcal. - (carb:70% / prot:30%)
100g.=48,26kcal. / protein 3,93g. fat:5,09g.
µg. - Ph:3,72 Na:0,77 Ka:23,54 Mg:1,43 Ca:2 Fe:0,05 Zn:0,02 Col.:0 Hsr.:1,19

Quantity of ingredients:
Sesame oil 1 table spoon / 10g. (little)
Potato 4 pieces / 300g. (little)
Onion (spring onion) 3 pieces / 60g. (yes)
Pepper (ground) 1 pinch / 0,5g. ()
Nutmeg 1 pinch / 1g. (yes)
Salt 1 pinch / 1g. (little)
Lemon 1/2 piece / 25g. (yes)
Cucumber 2 pieces / 500g. (yes)
Cream, sweet 30% 1 table spoon / 10g. (little)
Dill 1 table spoon / 15g. (yes)

Cooking instructions:
Sauté sesame oil, chopped potatoes, plenty of spring onions in a hot pot; add pepper, a little nutmeg, salt, lemon juice, hot water, diced cucumber; simmer for about 10 minutes and then puree; add some sweet cream as you like,
and fresh dill.
Variation: Add a little chili, oregano, thyme or rosemary to soften the cooling effect.

9.38 Rice with parsnips

Rich in vitamins, minerals potassium and zinc. Good to fight blood circulation disorders, thrombose, risk of embolism, high blood pressure, a headache, heart attack and stroke, yeast infections.
Cooking time approx. 45 min
3 portions to 261,33g. / 206kcal. - (carb:78% / prot:22%)
100g.=78,95kcal. / protein 5,16g. fat:4,52g.
µg. - Ph:6,72 Na:0,7 Ka:31,66 Mg:2,54 Ca:3,53 Fe:0,05 Zn:0,07 Col.:0 Hsr.:4,06

Quantity of ingredients:
Rice variety any 1 cup / 120g. (yes)
Water 1 1/2 cups / 200g. (yes)
Salt 1 pinch / 1g. (little)
Parsnip 3-4 pieces / 450g. (yes)
Olive oil 1 table spoon / 10g. (yes)
Sage 1 teaspoon / 3g. (yes)

Cooking instructions:
Peel the parsnips and cut into slices. Fry for a short time in oil. Add the rice and fry again for a short time. Add the water and cook it at least 30 min. Sprinkle with fresh chopped sage.

9.39 Rice with stewed vegetables

Reduces blood pressure, strengthens immune system, prevents cancer, reduces radiation damage, extremely low fat content, good to fight blood circulation disorders, thrombose, risk of embolism, a headache, heart attack and stroke. Is diuretic.
Cooking time approx. 20 min
Allergens: L
2 portions to 310,5g. / 166kcal. - (carb:82% / prot:18%)
100g.=53,62kcal. / protein 4,33g. fat:2,25g.
µg. - Ph:8,31 Na:2,83 Ka:26,32 Mg:3,14 Ca:5,9 Fe:0,2 Zn:0,07 Col.:0 Hsr.:6,32

Quantity of ingredients:
Rice variety any 1/2 cup / 60g. (yes)
Water 3 cups / 300g. (yes)
Lemon peel 1 piece / 3g. (yes)
Water 1/2 cup / 0g. (yes)
Carrot 2 pieces / 180g. (yes)
Celery sticks 1/2 piece / 5g. (yes)
Champignon 1/2 cup / 50g. (little)
Cress 2 table spoons / 20g. (yes)
Linseed oil 1 dash / 3g. (yes)

Cooking instructions:
Cook rice according to basic recipe with a piece of lemon peel.
Steam chopped carrots, celery and mushrooms until soft.
Then sprinkle with cress. Then add a dash of high quality cold oil.

9.40 Rosemary Potatoes

Reduces Inflammation, improves digestion, regenerates skin, supports
urination, lowers cholesterol. Rosemary stimulates digestion,
strengthens lung, promotes spleen and kidney, dries out.
Cooking time approx. 30 min
2 portions to 216,5g. / 188kcal. - (carb:76% / prot:24%)
100g.=87,07kcal. / protein 4,21g. fat:5,25g.
μg. - Ph:11,51 Na:0,72 Ka:82,88 Mg:4,72 Ca:1,86 Fe:0,1 Zn:0,07 Col.:0 Hsr.:3,64

Quantity of ingredients:
Potato 6-8 pieces / 420g. (little)
Salt (herbal) 1 pinch / 1g. (little)
Olive oil 1 table spoon / 10g. (yes)
Rosemary 1 teaspoon / 2g. (yes)

Cooking instructions:
Cut the potatoes into half´s, apply a little olive oil on the cut surface,
then salt, sprinkle 2 - 3 rosemary needles on the potatoes.
Place the potatoes on the baking tray and bake them in the preheated
oven for approx. 25 minutes to 190°C/374°F.

9.41 Strawberry soup with melons

Relieves pain and inflammation in rheumatism. Diuretic, helps to fight
constipation.
Cooking time approx. 5 min
2 portions to 285,5g. / 87kcal. - (carb:86% / prot:14%)
100g.=30,47kcal. / protein 2,04g. fat:0,83g.
μg. - Ph:5,98 Na:1,54 Ka:50,58 Mg:3,39 Ca:5,16 Fe:0,14 Zn:0,01 Col.:0 Hsr.:6,68

Quantity of ingredients:
Strawberries 3/4 lbs / 300g. (little)
Strawberry Juice 1/3 cup / 70g. (little)
Lemon peel 1/4 teaspoon / 1g. (yes)

Cooking instructions:
Puree strawberries (fresh or frozen) and strawberry juice with the blender, mix in a little sugar.
Cut melon pulp into small pieces.
Arrange strawberry soup in portions. Put the melon cubes in the sweet soup.

9.42 Tea Black tea (Russian tea)

Black tea improves blood circulation.
Cooking time approx. 10 min
1 portion to 125g. / 7kcal. - (carb:3% / prot:97%)
100g.=5,6kcal. / protein 1,28g. fat:0,26g.
µg. - Ph:11,92 Na:1,2 Ka:72,32 Mg:7,96 Ca:16,52 Fe:0,07 Zn:0,1 Col.:0 Hsr.:13,12

Quantity of ingredients:
Black tea 1 table spoon / 5g. (little)
Water 1 cup / 120g. (yes)

Cooking instructions:
For each cup you use a teaspoonful or a teabag.
Pour green tea only with 60 to 80 ° C / 140 to 176 °F hot water, otherwise it will be bitter.
If the tea has a stimulating effect, let it draw for two to three minutes. It has a calming effect for a duration of five minutes (no longer, otherwise it will be bitter!).
Another method: Pour the tea leaves with about 70 ° C / 158 °F hot water and pour the water immediately again. Then just pour hot water again. The bitter substances disappear, and the tea gets a milder aroma.

9.43 Tea from ginger with honey

Honey relieves pain, detoxifying, bactericide.
Fresh ginger encourages digestion, detoxifying, strengthens bodily production, promotes perspiration, reduces blood lipids, stimulates, dissolves stagnation.
Cooking time approx. 30 min
4 portions to 127,25g. / 5kcal. - (carb:98% / prot:2%)
100g.=3,73kcal. / protein 0,01g. fat:0g.
µg. - Ph:0,02 Na:0,07 Ka:0,17 Mg:0,08 Ca:0,32 Fe:0 Zn:0,01 Col.:0 Hsr.:0

Quantity of ingredients:
Ginger fresh 1 teaspoon / 3g. (yes)
Water 2 cup / 500g. (yes)
Honey 2 teaspoons / 6g. (yes)

Cooking instructions:
Heat the water till it boils and put it aside. Add ginger and 20-30 min. to let go. Sweet to taste with honey.

9.44 Tea Green tea

Green tea promotes digestion, supports urination, dissolves mucus, detoxifying, stimulates nerves, reduces blood lipids, lowers cholesterol, reduces inflammation.
Cooking time approx. 10 min
1 portion to 122g. / 2kcal. - (carb:20% / prot:80%)
100g.=1,64kcal. / protein 0g. fat:0g.
µg. - Ph:5,61 Na:1,07 Ka:27,59 Mg:4,07 Ca:9,43 Fe:0,03 Zn:0,1 Col.:0 Hsr.:0

Quantity of ingredients:
Green tea 1 teaspoon / 2g. (yes)
Water 1 cup / 120g. (yes)

Cooking instructions:
For each cup you use a teaspoonful or a teabag.
Pour green tea only with 60 to 80 ° C / 140 to 176 °F hot water, otherwise it will be bitter.
If the tea has a stimulating effect, let it draw for two to three minutes. It has a calming effect for a duration of five minutes (no longer, otherwise it will be bitter!).
Another method: Pour the tea leaves with about 70 ° C / 158 °F hot water and pour the water immediately again. Then just pour hot water again. The bitter substances disappear, and the tea gets a milder aroma.

9.45 Thick pea soup

Supports urination, detoxifying, dissolves stagnation, improves blood circulation, strengthens liver and kidney, strengthens immune system.
Cooking time approx. 2-3 hours
Allergens: AN
3 portions to 255g. / 123kcal. - (carb:47% / prot:53%)
100g.=48,37kcal. / protein 4,36g. fat:7,3g.
µg. - Ph:3,44 Na:0,25 Ka:7,5 Mg:1,22 Ca:1,55 Fe:0,06 Zn:0,04 Col.:0 Hsr.:5,21

Quantity of ingredients:
Peas, green 3/8 lbs - 6oz / 150g. (little)
Water 2 1/4 cups / 550g. (yes)
Sesame oil 1 table spoon / 20g. (little)
Onion white 1/2 piece / 25g. (yes)
Ginger fresh 1/2 teaspoon / 1g. (yes)
Ground 1/2 teaspoon / 1g. (yes)
Oat meal 1 table spoon / 15g. (yes)
Salt 1 pinch / 1g. (little)
Parsley 1 stem / 2g. (yes)

Cooking instructions:
Soak dried peas before cooking. Sauté sesame oil, onion, a little oatmeal, ginger and cumin in a hot pot; add the peas and simmer for 2-3 hours; add salt at the end and purée with a blender; garnish with parsley.

9.46 Tomato soup

Promotes digestion, helps to digest fat, supports urination, reduces blood pressure, dissolves stagnation. Contains unsaturated fatty acids, is antioxidative.
Cooking time approx. 10 min
2 portions to 290g. / 100kcal. - (carb:42% / prot:58%)
100g.=34,66kcal. / protein 1,78g. fat:7,9g.
µg. - Ph:4,2 Na:1,2 Ka:31,36 Mg:1,99 Ca:3,85 Fe:0,07 Zn:0,04 Col.:0,01 Hsr.:1,47

Quantity of ingredients:
Olive oil 1 table spoon / 15g. (yes)
Onion white 1 piece / 60g. (yes)
Cinnamon ground 1 pinch / 1g. (little)
Basil (fresh) 1 teaspoon / 2g. (yes)
Pepper (ground) 1 pinch / 0,5g. ()
Salt 1 pinch / 1g. (little)
Tomato 6 pieces / 250g. (yes)
Water 5/8 lbs - 8oz / 250g. (yes)
Peppers powder 1 pinch / 1g. (little)

Cooking instructions:
Roast the onion in a pot. Salt and spices. Briefly roast. Put washed and quartered tomatoes in the pan. Stir and sauté briefly. Add a quart of water and heat till it boils. Cook for a quarter of an hour and puree.

9.47 Warming carrot soup

Strengthens and warms, reduces blood pressure, strengthens immune system, prevents cancer, reduces radiation damage, strengthens gastrointestinal function.
Cooking time approx. 30 min
Allergens: HL
3 portions to 274,67g. / 133kcal. - (carb:79% / prot:21%)
100g.=48,54kcal. / protein 2,16g. fat:7,86g.
µg. - Ph:2,86 Na:2,31 Ka:9,18 Mg:8,37 Ca:32,64 Fe:0,13 Zn:0,03 Col.:0 Hsr.:1

Quantity of ingredients:
Carrot 4 pieces / 250g. (yes)
Walnut oil 2 table spoons / 20g. (yes)
Onion (shallot) 2 pieces / 40g. (yes)
Anise (Common Fennel) 1/2 teaspoon / 1g. (yes)
Nutmeg 1 pinch / 1g. (yes)
Ginger fresh 1/2 teaspoon / 1g. (yes)
Salt 1 pinch / 1g. (little)
Basic recipe for a vegetable soup (nutritious) 2 cup / 500g. (little)
Parsley 1 table spoon / 10g. (yes)

Cooking instructions:
Heat walnut oil in a hot pot and fry onions; steam the carrots in it; add anise, nutmeg, a little ginger, salt and sauté everything; add water or vegetable- or meat stock; cook everything soft and then puree; fold in parsley at the end.

Recommendation: Suitable for the cold season, especially if you use meat broth as a liquid for infusion.

9.48 Zucchini semolina cream soup

Good to fight loss of appetite, reduces blood pressure, promotes weight loss. Good to fight loss of appetite, flatulence, inflammatory bowel disease, rheumatism, heartburn.
Cooking time approx. 25 min
Allergens: AGL
4 portions to 341,75g. / 146kcal. - (carb:78% / prot:22%)
100g.=42,72kcal. / protein 4,02g. fat:7,8g.
µg. - Ph:1,7 Na:0,83 Ka:9,09 Mg:4,88 Ca:18,35 Fe:0,08 Zn:0,02 Col.:0,22 Hsr.:0,82

Quantity of ingredients:
Butter organic 1/2 oz / 20g. (yes)
Wheat semolina 2 table spoons / 20g. (yes)
Parsley 1 Bunch / 100g. (yes)
Basic recipe for a vegetable soup (nutritious) 3 1/2 cups / 800g. (little)
Lovage 1/2 teaspoon / 2g. (yes)
Nutmeg 1 pinch / 0,5g. (yes)
Anise (Common Fennel) 1 pinch / 0,5g. (yes)
Zucchini 7/8 lbs / 400g. (yes)
Ginger fresh 1/2 teaspoon / 1g. (yes)
Crème fraiche cheese 2 table spoons / 20g. (little)
Lemon peel 1/4 piece / 2g. (yes)
Salt 1 pinch / 1g. (little)
Pepper (ground) 1 pinch / 0,5g. ()

Cooking instructions:
Melt the butter in a saucepan, add the semolina and fry briefly while stirring. Add half of the chopped parsley, sauté for a short time, pour vegetable broth according to the basic recipe, season with chopped lovage, nutmeg and anise. Cook the soup without lid lightly for 10 minutes. Add the finely chopped zucchini and the small piece of lemon zest, cook gently for 5 minutes until the zucchini are tender. Remove the lemon peel.
Using the blender, finely puree the soup with the crème fraiche and the remaining parsley.

10 Effects of food

10.1 Use ingredients: recommendable

Acai powder
Bitter Herb liqueur
Cream 10% coffee cream
Fox nut, gorgon nut, makhana
Fresh cheese from soya

Hibiscus
Kudzu
Lily bulbs
Mascarpone cheese

10.2 Use ingredients: yes

Adzuki beans
Agar agar (kelp)
Agave nectar
Angelica root
Anise (Common Fennel)
Arrowroot
Artichoke
Asparagus (green or white)
Aubergine
Avocado
Balm
Bamboo shoots
Banchatee (green tea)
barberry
Barley
Barley flour
Barley grass powder
Barley grouts
Barley malt
Barley not peeled
Basil
Basil (fresh)
Batavia
Bay leaf
Bearberry leaf
Bitter Lemon
Bitter orange peel
Black caraway
Blackberry leaves
Blue mallow tee
Borage
Borage oil
Boxhorn clover seeds
Bread roll
Bread with carob kernel flour
Breadcrumbs (wheat bread, bread roll)
Buckbean
Buckwheat
Buckwheat (roasted) Kasha
Buckwheat whole grain
Bulgur (cereals)

Burdock root tea
Butter (half fat)
Butter organic
Capers in olive oil
Carob flour, St. john's bread
Carrot
Carrot (Early Carrot)
Carrot juice without sugar
Cauliflower
Celery root
Celery sticks
Cereal coffee
Chamomile
Chamomile tea
Chervil
Chervil dried
Chicken egg
Chicken egg white
Chicken meat
Chicken yolk
Chicory
Chili (pod or ground)
Chives
Chlorella (fresh water)
Chrysanthemum blossom tea
Cinnamon sticks
Clarified butter
Clove
Coconut flakes
Coconut grated
Coconut meat
Coconut milk
Cooking oil
Coriander
Coriander (fresh)
Corn
Corn (fast polenta)
Corn (roasted)
Corn flour
Corn germ oil
Corn Grease (Polenta)

Corn silk tea
Corn starch
Couscous
Cream sour 10%
Creamer
Cress
Crispbread
Cucumber
Cucumber (bitter)
Cucumber (spicy cucumber)
Cumin (Caraway seed)
Curcuma
Curry
Curry paste red
Daisy
Dandelion (young plants)
Dandelion juice
Dandelionroots tea
Dashi
Dates dried
Dates red
Dill
Dyer's broom herb
Elderberry blossom tee
Endive salad
Evening primrose oil
Fennel
Fennel seeds ground
Fennel tea
Fenugreek (Trigonella foenum-graecum)
Flounder
Flower pollen
Fresh cheese with herbs
Fructose (glucose)
Fruit mix juice
Garam Masala powder
Garlic
Gelee Royal
Gentian root
Gentian root tea
Ginger fresh
Ginger oil
Ginger powder
Ginseng
Ginseng root
Gourd
Grapefruit (Pomelo)
Grapefruit dried peel
Grapefruit juice
Green tea
Ground
Ground caraway
Hawthorn

Herbal tea mix
Herbs bitter
Herbs of Provence
Herbs various
Herbs wild
Hibiscus tea
Hokkaido pumpkin
Honey
Horehound leaves
Hyssop
Iceberg lettuce
Jasmine blossoms tee
Juniper berry
King Solomon's-seal
Kukicha tea
Kumquats
Lamb's lettuce
Lavender blossoms
Leaf salads (bitter)
Leek
Lemon
Lemon Balm (dried)
Lemon Balm (fresh)
Lemon juice
Lemon peel
Lemongrass
Lettuce
Licorice root tea
Lime
Lime blossom tea
Linseed oil
Liver smoothing tea
Lotus roots
Lotus seeds
Lovage
Lovage seeds
Luo Han Guo fruit
Lye roll
Mallow (Malva sylvestris) blossom tea
Malt
Maple syrup
Margarine
Margarine (diet)
Marjoram
Millet
Millet flakes
Mulled Wine Spice
Multi-grain bread (gray bread)
Nasturtium (nose-twister or nose-tweaker)
Nettles
Noodles (wheat) with egg
Noodles (wheat, lasagne) with egg
Noodles (wheat, ribbon noodles) with

egg
Noodles (wheat, spaghetti) with egg
Noodles (whole grain) with egg
Nori, purple seaweed, red algae
Nutmeg
Oat
Oat flakes (whole grain)
Oat flakes roasted
Oat flour
Oat fusion (baby food)
Oat meal
Olive oil
Olives green
Onion (shallot)
Onion (spring onion)
Onion read
Onion white
Orange
Oregano dried
Oregano fresh
Palm oil
Parsley
Parsley root
Parsnip
Passion blossoms tea
Pearl barley
Pearl barley
Pepper (ground)
Pepper Cayenne
Pepper white (ground)
Peppercorns
Peppermint
Peppermint tea
Pepperoni
Pepperoni, red, pitted, halved
Pepperoni, yellow, pitted, halved
Peppers
Peppers (rose peppers)
Peppers (sweet)
Pickle
Psyllium seed
Pudding powder vanilla
Puff pastry
Pumpkin
Pumpkin seed oil
Radicchio
Radish
Radish (white, green, purple-red)
Radish black
Radish horseradish
Radish leaves
Rapeseed oil
Raspberry leaf tea
Red beet

Red berry (without sugar)
Ribworttea
Rice (fragrance)
Rice (Gaoliang / Sorghum)
Rice (whole grain)
Rice Basmati
Rice black
Rice flour
Rice long grain rice
Rice malt
Rice mash
Rice noodles
Rice red
Rice round grain
Rice starch
Rice sticky
Rice sweet
Rice variety any
Rice wild (nature rice)
Rose blossom tea
Rose leaf tea
Rosemary
Rusk
Rye
Rye flour
Safflower (Dyer's thistle / Hong Hua)
Sage
Sago (cereals)
Salsify
Sourdough
Spelled flakes
Spelled grain
Spelled semolina
Spurdog (spiny dogfish, Schillerlocken)
St. Benedict's thistle, blessed thistle,
holy thistle, spotted thistle
Strawberry jam
Sugar - icing sugar
Sugar brown
Sugar candy white
Sugar cane sugar
Sugar fructose - fruit sugar
Sugar glucose - grapes sugar
Sugar Milk Sugar
Sugar molasses
Sugar palm sugar
Sugar substitute (sweetener)
Sugar white
Tarragon (Estragon)
Tea mixture uric acid lowering
Thistle oil
Thyme
Thyme dried
Tomato

Tomato puree
Tsampa (roasted barley flour)
Umeboshi paste
Umeboshi plums (Japanese apricots)
Valerian
Vanilla
Vanilla pod
Vanilla powder
Vanilla sugar natural
Vinegar (Apple vinegar)
Vinegar (Red wine vinegar)
Vinegar Aceto Balsamico
Vinegar Aceto Balsamico white
Walnut oil
Water
Water hot
Watermelon
Wax gourd
Wheat
Wheat bulgur
Wheat flakes
Wheat flatbread/pita bread
Wheat flour
Wheat germ oil

Wheat semolina
Wheat semolina for children
Wheatgrass juice
Wheatgrass powder
White bread (baguette)
White bread (pretzel sticks)
White bread (roll)
White bread (wheat bread)
White breadcrumbs
White dumpling bread (wheat bread cut into chunks)
Wild garlic (garlic spinach)
Wild herbs
Wild strawberries
Wormwood herb
Yam root, yam root tuber
Yarrow
Yarrow tea
Yoghurt vanilla
Yogi tea
Yogurt (natural, 1.5% fat)
Yogurt (natural, 3.5% fat)
Zucchini

10.3 Use ingredients: little

Acerola fruit nectar or powder
Aloe juice
Amaranth
Amaranth Pops
Anchovy / Sardine
Apple (sour)
Apple (sweet)
Apple puree
Apricot
Apricot jam
Apricots
Baking powder
Basic recipe for a beef soup
Basic recipe for a beef soup (warming)
Basic recipe for a chicken soup (warming)
Basic recipe for a duck soup
Basic recipe for a fish soup
Basic recipe for a rice soup (Congee)
Basic recipe for a vegetable soup (nutritious)
Bean oil
Beans (green, fresh)
Beef bone marrow
Beef fillet
Beef heart

Beef heart (calf)
Beef kidney
Beef liver
Beef lungs (calf)
Beef meat
Beef meat (calf)
Beef meatbones
Beef Oxtail pieces
Beef soup meat
Beef stomach
Berries of the season
Bitter liqueur
Black beans
Black fungus mushroom
Black tea
Blackberry dried (unripe fruit)
Blackberry jam
Blackberry´s
Black-eyed peas
Blackthorn (Sloe)
Blueberry
Blueberry dried
Blueberry jam
Bocksdorn fruits (Fructus Lycii, Goji, goji berry dried
Brazil nuts

Brie cheese
Broad beans (thick beans)
Broccoli
Brown ale
Brussels sprouts
Bush beans
Butter beans white
Buttermilk
Calamari
Camembert
Campari
Cantaloupe
Carambola (Star fruit)
Cardamom
Carp
Cashews
Caviar
Champignon
Channa-Dal
Chenpi (chinese tangerine bowl)
Cherry
Cherry (sour)
Cherry compote
Chestnut puree
Chestnuts
Chicken Blood
Chicken heart
Chicken liver
Chicken stomach
Chickpeas
Chickweed
Chinese cabbage
Chinese pearl barley
Cinnamon ground
Clementine
Clementines
Cocoa
Coconut fat
Cod
Codfish
Coffee
Coix (seeds) YiYi Ren
Compote (fruits of the season)
Cottage cheese
Cow's milk (1.5% fat)
Cow's milk (whole milk 3.5% fat)
Crab
Cranberries
Cranberry
Cranberry
Cranberry jam
Cranberry juice
Cream (30% fat)
Cream sour 20%

Cream sour 30%
Cream, sweet 30%
Créme fraiche cheese
Crucian
Curd cheese 20%
Curd cheese 40%
Currant (black)
Currant (red)
Currant (white)
Currant jam (black)
Currant jam (red)
Deer meat
Deer meat
Deer's Bones
Deer's kidneys
Duck (heart)
Duck (slaughtered)
Ducks egg
Dulse (seaweed)
Edam cheese
Eel
Eel smoked
Elderberries
Fernet Branca (herbal bitter liqueur)
Feta cheese
Feta cheese
Fig
Fish innards
Fish pieces mixed (fresh water)
Fish remains
Fish sauce
French beans
Fresh cheese
Freshwater crab
Freshwater fish
Gail plum
Galangal
Gelatin white
Ginkgo fruit
Ginseng liqueur
Goat
Goat and sheep's blood
Goat and sheep's brain
Goat and sheep's liver
Goat and sheep's milk
Goat and sheep's stomach
Goat cheese
Goose
Goose blood
Goose egg
Goose fat
Goose parts
Gooseberry
Gorgonzola

Gouda cheese
Grape juice red
Grape juice white
Grapes red
Grapes white
Grapeseed oil
Grass carp
Green spelt
Greengage
Guava
Halibut (Flatfish)
Herring
Hijiki
Honey wine (Met)
Hop
Horse meat
Jellyfish
Kaki plum
Kalmus
Kefir
Kidney beans (red)
Kiwi
Kohlrabi
Kombu seaweed (Saccharina japonica)
Ladyfingers
Lamb bones
Lamb kidneys
Lamb liver
Lamb meat
Lamb shoulder
Lamb's lettuce
Lentils
Lentils black
Lentils red
Lentils yellow
Lima beans
Linseed
Linseed (crushed)
Lobster
Longane
Loquate / Japanese medlar
Lychee
Lychee in Preserved
Lychee liqueur
Mackerel
Mango
Mango juice
Manioc flour
Mare's milk
Martini
Mayonnaise 50%
Mayonnaise 80%
Mediterranean fish (cod, plaice,
haddock, sea eel, mackerel)

Medlar
Mirabelle plum
Miso
Miso black (fermented)
Miso paste (soy bean paste)
Mixed Pickles
Mold cheese
Morel (black, dried)
Morel, dried
Mozzarella
Mu Erh Mushroom
Muesli
Mulberry fruit
Mullet
Mung bean
Mung bean sprouting
Mussels
Mustard
Mustard Dijon
Mustard medium hot
Mustard seeds
Mustard sweet
Mutton
Mutton
Nectarine
Oat milk
Octopus
Octopus
Okra
Olives
Orange blossom
Orange dried peel
Orange grated peel
Orange jam
Orange peel
Oyster shell powder
Papaya
Passion fruit
Peaches
Peaches (canned)
Peanut (roasted)
Peanut butter
Peanut oil
Peanuts
Pear
Peas
Peas, green
Pepper powder (hot)
Peppers powder
Perch
Pheasant
Pig blood
Pigeon
Pigeon egg

Pimento
Pine nuts
Pineapple
Pineapple juice without sugar
Pinto beans speckled
Plaice
Plum
Plums
Pomegranate
Pork Bacon
Pork brain
Pork fat (lard)
Pork ham
Pork ham cooked
Pork ham smoked
Pork heart
Pork kidneys
Pork knuckle
Pork Lard
Pork liver
Pork lung
Pork marrow bones
Pork meat
Pork skin
Pork stomach
Pork/beef sausage (smoked)
Pork's intestine
Potato
Potato (mealy)
Potato flour
Prickly pear
Prosecco
Pumpernickel (dark bread)
Pumpkin seeds
Quail
Quail egg
Quince
Quinoa
Rabbit
Rabbit (wild)
Rabbit liver
Rabbit meat
Raspberry
Raspberry dried (immature)
Raspberry jam
Red cabbage
Reishi mushroom
Rhubarb
Romaine lettuce / lettuce salad
Rose hip
Rose hip tea
Rosefish
Rucola
Rum

Rye wholemeal bread
Saffron
Sake
Salmon
Salt
Salt (herbal)
Sauerkraut (cutted cabbage fermented)
Savory
Savoy cabbage / kale
Sea buckthorn
Sea cucumber
Seacrab
Sesame oil
Sesame oil roasted
Shark
Sheep's milk
Sheep's milk yoghurt
Sherry (whine)
Shrimp
Shrimps
Skim milk powder
Slug
Sorrel
Sour cherries
Sour cream 15% fat
Sour milk
Sour milk cheese 20%
Soy flour
Soy noodles
Soy sauce
Soy Tofu
Soy Tofu smoked
Soya Cuisine (soy cream)
Soybean milk
Soybean oil
Soybeans
Soybeans, black
Soybeans, blacks, fermented
Soybeans, yellow
Spelled (Dark) bread
Spelled wholemeal flour
Spiny lobsters
Spirit
Star anise
Stevia (candyleaf, sweetleaf)
Strawberries
Strawberry Juice
Sunflower oil
Sweet potato
Tabasco
Tangerine
Toast bread (whole grain)
Tomato dried
Tomato juice

44

Tomato paste
Tonic Water
Topinambur
Trout
Truffle
Tuna
Turkey breast meat
Turkey ham
Turmeric (yellow root)
Turnip
Turnips
Vegetable juice
Wakame
Walnuts
Walnuts roasted

Wheat beer
Wheat bran
Wheat flour whole grain
Wheat/Rye/Gray-black bread with yeast
Whey
White beans
White cabbage
White wine
Whitefish
Whole grain bread
Wholemeal flour
Wild boar meat
Wormwood
Yeast
Yew nut

10.4 Do not use contra-acting foods

Agrimony
Almond
Almond marzipan
Almond milk
Almond puree
Apple juice (natural cloudy)
Apricot dried
Apricot nectar
Apricots juice
Banana
Banana (cooking banana)
Beer (alcohol-free)
Beer (alcohol-reduced)
Beer (Pils)
Beer (Top-fermented German dark beer)
Berry juice
Blueberry juice
Boletus mushroom
Chanterelle
Chard
Cherry juice
Chocolate
Chocolate (Diabetic)
Cola drink
Cola drink (low calorie)
Currant juice (black)
Currants (black)

Currants (red)
Emmental cheese
Fig dried
Fruit tea
Hazelnuts
Mineral water
Orange juice
Oyster mushroom
Oysters
Parmesan
Pear juice
Pineapple (from a can)
Pistachios
Plum dried
Poppy
Pork sausage (Bratwurst)
Processed cheese 12%
processed cheese 30%
Raisins
Red wine
Sesame paste (Tahini)
Sesame, black
Sesame, white
Shiitake, dried
Spinach
Sunflower seeds
Supplementary nutrition
Trout (smoked)

11 Basics of Nutrition

The basic principles of nutrition described herein are general recommendations. They are not aimed at a specific form of therapy. Recommendations concerning a therapy have priority.

11.1 Nutrition

Regular meals in a relaxed atmosphere. A warm breakfast is considered a good start into the day.
The main meals ought to be taken for lunch – supper in the early evening. Pay attention to feeling hungry or sated: don't eat too much nor remain hungry is the rule
Prepare the meals freshly from natural, regional products. Frozen, heat-conserved, industrially prepared or foodstuffs cooked in the microwave oven are rejected.
Choice of foodstuffs according to the season: more cooling food in summer, more warming food in winter.
Eat cooked food at least twice a day. Food and drinks ought to be lukewarm, never ice-cold or hot.
Raw vegetables, briefly cooked vegetables, freshly squeezed juices and mineral water are not recommended. Milk and dairy products are only included in the diet if they don't cause problems.
Don't use therapeutic recipes over a longer period without consulting your doctor or therapist.

Varied food
Enjoy the diversity of foodstuffs. Characteristics of a balanced nutrition are variety, suitable combination and a balanced quantity of rich and low energy foodstuffs (on one hand avoiding undersupply with essential nutrients and on the other hand to take to many undesirable substances).

A lot of Cereal Products - and Potatoes
Bread, pasta, rice, cereal flakes (best wholemeal) as well as potatoes contain almost no fat, but many vitamins, mineral nutrients, trace elements, roughage and secondary plant substances. These foodstuffs ought to be taken with low-fat side dishes.

Vegetables and Fruit – „Take Five" every day …
5 portions of vegetables and fruit a day, as fresh as possible, briefly cooked, or maybe one portion as a juice – ideal as a side dish to every meal as well as snack between meals: Thus a lot of vitamins, mineral nutrients as well as roughage and secondary plant substances

Daily milk and dairy products
Milk and Dairy Products every Day, once or twice per Week Fish; meat, sausages as well as eggs moderately. These foodstuffs contain valuable nutrients like calcium in the milk, iodine selenium and omega-3 fat acids in saltwater fish. Meat is favorable due to its high content of disposable iron and the vitamins B1, B6 and B12. Quantities of 300 – 600 g meat and sausage per week are sufficient. Prefer low-fat products, especially in meat- and dairy products.

Low-fat and fatty Foodstuffs
Fat supplies us with essential fat acids and fatty foodstuffs contain also fat-soluble vitamins. Fat is high in energy; therefore much fat in the food may cause overweight, possibly also cancer. Too many saturated fat acids may further a tendency for cardio-vascular diseases in the long term. Prefer vegetable oils and fats (e.g. rapeseed-, olive-, soya-oils and solid fats produced therefrom). Beware of invisible fat in meat- and dairy products, pastry and sweets as well as in fast-food and convenience foods. 70 – 90 g fat per day is sufficient.

Moderately Sugar and Salt
Take sugar and foods/drinks containing various kinds of sugar (e.g. glucose syrup) only occasionally. Use herbs and spices as well as a little salt creatively. Prefer salt containing iodine.

Plenty of Liquids
Water is absolutely essential. Drink 1-2 l liquids every day. Prefer water (with or without gas) and other low-calorie drinks. Alcoholic drinks should not be taken.

Tasty Dishes, carefully cooked
Cook the meals with as low temperatures and as short as possible, using little water and fat – this preserves the original taste, keeps the nutrients intact and prevents the production of harmful compounds.

Take time and enjoy the food
Take your Time and enjoy your Food
Eating consciously helps to eat right. The eye enjoys food, too. It's fun, invites to enjoy varied dishes and stimulates the feeling of satiety.

Watch your Weight and stay in Motion
A balanced diet and a lot of exercise and sport (30 – 60 min/day) are a healthy combination. The right weight furthers well-being and health. Thermals, directional effectiveness, digestive power

There are various criteria for judging the effectiveness of herbs and foodstuffs.

The use of certain herbs and ingredients is based on observations of the effects on the body which these foodstuffs, herbs and spices show after having eaten them. The medical science has developed following system: Every ingredient or herb has a directional effectiveness. Furthermore, there are herbs which have a special effect on certain organs.

The basic condition for a healthy metabolism is to obtain sufficient energy from food and that the digestive process doesn't use too much energy. An easily digestible meal makes content and sated, doesn't cause flatulence and fatigue after the meal. The perfect spices increase the healthiness of our meals. Very often, just small doses of herbs and spices will suffice. They are not used to make us sated, but to help our digestive organs to digest the food.

11.2 Recipes

The recipes list the ingredients to be used and the cooking instructions show how the dish is prepared. The list of ingredients shows the concerned quantities as well as the relevance for the therapy. If you find „less than mentioned", try to comply or find an alternative from the „list of recommended foodstuffs". Mostly it shall result just in a small change of taste when you simply avoid this ingredient.

Mild cooking methods: boiling, stewing, poaching, steaming
Strong cooking methods: barbecuing, roasting, frying, smoking
Balanced cooking methods: deep-frying, baking brick
Deep-freezing and warming in the microwave oven should be avoided (denaturalization).

11.3 Foodstuffs

Foodstuffs have an effect on body and soul like medicinal herbs, only a very much milder one. Dietary advice is mainly based on regional foodstuffs. The knowledge about the effects of each foodstuff and the knowledge, when which foodstuff shall be used, is based on the orthodox school of medicine. Use ecologic-organic products, if possible. As everything should be cooked for a long time due to a better digestability and very rarely eaten raw, the food agrees with everyone.

The classification of the foodstuffs according to their effect on the body is the basis in order to achieve a harmonious status of health.

Dietary advisors do not recommend certain foodstuffs for everyone. The individual diet is tailor-made for the individual constitution.

Buy only fresh and ripe fruit and vegetables. You ought to leave unripe fruit and vegetables and such with brown spots and wilted leaves behind in the market. In this case take deep-frozen goods (never ready-to-serve dishes!). Fruit and vegetables are deep-frozen immediately after harvesting and often contain more vitamins and minerals than the goods from the vegetable shelf. Whereas conserved or tinned goods contain very much less biological substances. Also, salt, sugar and others are mostly added to the latter. Never leave the foodstuffs in the water after washing them to avoid that many vital substances get drowned. Clean salads, fruit and vegetables immediately before serving.

Please make sure of the hygienic processing of foodstuffs. Clean your salads, fruit and vegetables carefully. When cooking with meat, prepare all ingredients first and then process the meat products. Clean the worktop and tools very carefully. Wooden surfaces ought to be treated with a mild disinfectant regularly in order to reduce germination.

Store fruit and vegetables separately, if possible. Harvested fruit and vegetables are still alive and emit e.g. ethylene gas, which makes other products ripen and age faster. Keep meat and fish in the closed packaging or store them in the fridge in closed containers.

11.4 Herbs

There are some basic rules for storing medicinal herbs. On principle, herbs must be protected from direct sunlight, humidity and heat.

Containers for the storage of herbs may be glasses, ceramic jars and even plastic containers. However, plastic is a rather unsuitable material and should only be a short-term solution. In case of glass containers, use a dark material.

Medicinal herbs cannot be kept for any long period. The shelf life of herbs is limited. However, it can be prolonged with suitable storage. The place should be dark, rather cool and absolutely dry. A wooden medicine cabinet, placed not directly next to a source of heat, would be ideal. Never buy large quantities of herbs so as not to have to throw them away. Label the container with the name of the herb and the date of harvesting or processing.

12 Other dietic-books

The following syndromes of dietetics, TCM or for a therapy supplement for cancer are available.

Dietetics

E001. Nutrition of the infant - baby food
E002. Nutrition during lactation
E003. Nutrition in old age
E004. Nutrition of children and adolescents
E005. Nutrition of athletes
E006. Light weight
E007. Pregnancy
E008. Full food

Protein and electrolyte - kidneys
E009. (hemodialysis) dialysis treatment
E010. Acute renal failure
E011. Chronic renal insufficiency
E012. Nephrotic syndrome
E013. Kidney stones (nephrolithiasis)

Gastrointestinal tract - pancreas
E014. Acute pancreatitis (inflammation of the pancreas)
E015. Chronic pancreatitis (inflammation of the pancreas)

Gastrointestinal tract - small intestine and large intestine
E016. Acute obstipation (constipation)
E017. Chronic obstipation (constipation)
E018. Colon irritabile
E019. Diverticulitis
E020. Acquired lactose intolerance (lactose malabsorption)
E021. Fructose malabsorption
E022. Glutensensitive enteropathy (celiac disease)
E023. Colectomy
E024. Short Bowel Syndrome

Gastrointestinal tract - liver, gallbladder, bile ducts
E025. Acute and chronic hepatitis (inflammation of the liver)
E026. Cholelithiasis (bile stones)
E027. fatty liver
E028. cirrhosis

Gastrointestinal tract - Stomach and duodenal intestine
E029. Acute gastritis
E030. Chronic gastritis
E031. Stomach bleeding
E032. Ulcus ventriculi and duodenal ulcer
E033. Condition after gastric surgery

Gastrointestinal tract - oral cavity and esophagus
E034. Stomatitis
E035. Esophageal carcinoma (esophageal cancer)
E036. Refluosophagitis (heartburn)

Special diseases
E037. Phenylketonuria (PKU)
E038. Rheumatic joint diseases

Metabolism
E039. Obesity (overweight)
E040. Diabetes mellitus
E041. Eating disorders (underweight)

Fat metabolism
E042. Hypercholesterolaemia (increased cholesterol level)
E043. Hepatic Encephalopathy

Heart and circulation
E044. Arteriosclerosis (arterial calcification)
E045. Heart insufficiency
E046. Hypertension
E047. Hyperuricaemia and gout

Changed nutrient requirements
E048. In case of fever
E049. For malignant diseases
E050. After burns
E051. Radiation and chemotherapy

CANCER
E100. Pancreatic cancer
E101. Bladder cancer
E102. Blood cancer (leukemia)
E103. Breast cancer
E104. Colorectal cancer
E105. Gastric cancer
E106. Kidney cancer
E107. Esophageal cancer

TCM
E200. Bladder - moisture heat in the bladder
E201. Bladder - moisture and cold in the bladder
E202. Bladder - emptiness and cold in the bladder
E203. Large intestine - external cold affects the large intestine
E204. Large intestine - moisture heat in the large intestine
E205. Large intestine - heat blocks the intestine II acute
E206. Large intestine - dryness of the colon
E207. Large intestine - Yang deficiency (cold)
E208. Heart - Blood insufficiency
E209. Heart - Blood stagnation
E210. Heart - Fire
E211. Heart - Hot mucus clogs the heart pores

E212. Heart - Cold mucus clogs the heart pores
E213. Heart - Qi deficiency
E214. Heart - Yang deficiency
E215. Heart - Yin deficiency
E216. Liver - Ascending Liver Yang
E217. Liver - Blood deficiency
E218. Liver - Blood stagnation
E219. Liver - Moisture heat in liver and gall bladder
E220. Liver - Fire
E221. Liver - Gall bladder Qi-Empty
E222. Liver - Cold in the liver meridian
E223. Liver - Qi stagnation
E224. Liver - Wind
E225. Liver - Wind with ascending liver Yang
E226. Liver - Wind with blood anemic
E227. Liver - Wind with extreme heat
E228. Lung - Qi deficiency
E229. Lung - Mucus-moisture in the lungs
E230. Lung - Mucus-heat in the lungs
E231. Lung - Mucus-cold in the lungs
E232. Lung - Dryness of the lungs
E233. Lung - Wind-heat attacks the lungs
E234. Lung - Wind-cold affects the lungs
E235. Lung - Yin deficiency
E236. Stomach - Bloodstagnation
E237. Stomach - Fire
E238. Stomach - Cold with liquid
E239. Stomach - Nutrition stagnation
E240. Stomach - Qi deficiency
E241. Stomach - Rebellious Qi
E242. Stomach - Yin Emptiness
E243. Spleen - Heat and moisture attack the spleen
E244. Spleen - Coldness and moisture affects the spleen
E245. Spleen - Qi deficiency
E246. Spleen - Qi deficiency + Declining spleen Qi
E247. Spleen - Qi deficiency + spleen does not control the blood
E248. Spleen - Yang deficiency
E249. Kidney - Heart and kidney no longer communicate
E250. Kidney - Jing deficiency
E251. Kidney - Kidneys cannot receive the Qi
E252. Kidney - Qi is not stable
E253. Kidney - Yang deficiency
E254. Kidney - Yin deficiency

For further information visit di-book.com.

13 EBNS - Software for nutritional counseling

The main task of the database is to create personalized nutritional advice
for each patient individually. The database was developed for Dietetics

and Traditional Chinese Medicine.
The Database supports training and advices in the daily work routine.

The computer program provides lists of recipes, ingredients and herbs, which are given to the client. individually adjustable according to patient's request from whole food to vegetarians (lacto, ovo, ...). For every register there is an information sheet which can be given to the client. All texts can be individually designed.

The syndromes can be combined and result in an intersection of the recommended recipes and ingredients. The automated diagnosis for the TCM enables you to check your experience during the training as well as to confirm your diagnosis in the working day. You select several predefined symptoms and have the program automatically display the relevant syndromes.

How to work with the database:
Select the patient / client, select one or more of the syndromes you diagnosed and print the folder.

You can change all values, create new symptoms or syndromes, develop recipes, change or adapt ingredients and herbs to your findings. In simple client management, all relevant data about the person is stored. You get an overview of the past diagnoses and the development of the course of the disease.

As a consultant you save a lot of time when you print out the recipe, food and herbal lists for the recognized syndromes and give them to the clients. You can use this time for a personal conversation. With the database, dieticians and nutritionists can view the nutrients and trace elements for each recipe and develop recipes for syndromes even with suggested ingredients.

All recipe and grocery lists can also be ordered from me as a combination of several diseases. I wish all readers good luck, health and happiness in life.
More information can be found at www.ebns.at.
Volunteer: www.krebsinfo.at
Josef Miligui